Celebrations

Kate Tucker

A & C BLACK · LONDON

Series consultant: Julia Stanton

Thanks to the pupils, teachers and parents from St Mary Magdalene
Primary School for taking part in the photo shoots.
Thanks also to Joe Knight and Emma Lewin for lending props.

A CIP record for this book is available from the British Library.

ISBN 978-0-7136-6845-2

Reprinted 2007
First published 2004 by A & C Black Publishers Limited
38 Soho Square, London W1D 3HB
www.acblack.com

Contents

Introduction

The Foundation Stage begins at three years old, when most children will attend some form of pre-school or nursery. These early years are critical in children's education, and the government's **Early Learning Goals** provide an indication of the skills most children should develop by the end of the Foundation Stage, which is the end of the primary school Reception year.

The Early Learning Goals cover the following areas:

- Personal, social and emotional development
- Communication, language and literacy
- Mathematical development
- Knowledge and understanding of the world
- Physical development
- Creative development

In order to achieve the Early Learning Goals, there are four levels of learning, called **Stepping Stones**. These show the knowledge, skills, understanding and attitudes that children need to develop during the Foundation Stage. Children must show progression through the Stepping Stones in order to achieve the Early Learning Goals.

The Stepping Stones have been colour coded in this pack, in line with the Foundation Stage curriculum. Yellow indicates the expected learning level at the start of the Foundation Stage and grey indicates the expected level at the end of the Foundation Stage.

- YELLOW
- BLUE
- GREEN
- GREY

The Foundations Series

Foundations is a series of activity packs written for all adults working with children at the Foundation Stage across a range of settings: local authority nurseries; nursery centres; playgroups; pre-schools; accredited child-minders in approved child-minding networks; maintained schools or schools in the independent, private or voluntary sectors.

Each **Foundations** pack contains imaginative activities written specifically for those working with the Early Learning Goals and Stepping Stones. Each activity is tried and tested for suitability with children aged three to five, i.e. children at the Foundation Stage. Each book uses a popular early years theme and contains at least 40 activities that use the theme as a starting point for activities across the six key learning areas. There are also some groups of activities, such as 'Weddings' on pages 14-15, which encourage children to explore one element within the **Celebrations** theme in more detail.

Celebrations contains all you need to plan, organise and successfully lead activities on this theme. The activities are complemented by the following resources:
- a CD of songs, poems and stories, which are integral to the activities
- a giant wall poster, which can be used for display and as a useful stimulus for many of the activities
- eight colour photocards for use with various activities, or as stand-alone resources
- photocopiable sheets of resources, practical tasks and games to use with the activities
- ideas for displays and festival calendar which provides more background information.

Planning and assessment

This pack provides comprehensive coverage of the Early Learning Goals and includes a planning chart to help you organise your teaching. In addition, each activity highlights which Stepping Stones are covered.

During the course of the activities, children should be assessed regularly to ensure that they develop the skills required to progress through the Stepping Stones and achieve the Early Learning Goals. The following tips will help you to plan and compile assessment records for the children.

● Keep planning and assessment records for each of the children you teach. These records can be used at the end of the Foundation Stage to produce a brief report of the child's achievements against the Early Learning Goals and Stepping Stones. The child's next teacher will find this report particularly useful if it includes the themes covered.

● Each activity covers different Stepping Stones. This allows you to cnoose activities which are at the correct level for the children in your group, and also provides opportunities for assessment by outcome from the activity. Use the Early Learning Goals planning chart (pages 8-9) to ensure you are covering a range of areas of learning.

● Observe what the children do and say while they are working on the activities.

● Talk to them about what they are doing. Ask questions that give the children the opportunity to give open-ended answers, and to suggest what else they might do. You can use the questions suggested with each activity for extra help.

● As part of the assessment process, keep parents and carers informed of the work their child is doing. This pack includes ideas for improving home-school links (pages 32-33) and contains suggestions for activities that can be done at home.

How to use this pack

INTRODUCTION

The text in bold explains the purpose of the activity and outlines some expected outcomes.

QUESTIONS

Each activity has a prompt box of questions you could ask the children during the activity.

RESOURCES

This box lists the resources you will need for each activity.

Resources included in the pack are represented by an icon. These could be one of the following:
- Poster
- Activity Sheet
- Photocard
- CD

EARLY LEARNING GOALS

This heading indicates the main Early Learning Goal upon which the activity focuses. (See pages 8-9 for other Early Learning Goals which are also covered).

STEPPING STONES

These are key skills which the activity develops. The colour of the text indicates the corresponding Stepping Stone level in the Foundation Stage curriculum (see page 4).

KEY WORDS

This box contains key vocabulary that the children will encounter in the course of the activity.

INSTRUCTIONS

Follow the step by step instructions to find out how to prepare and carry out the activities.

EXTENSION

Some activities feature a further activity that extends and consolidates the children's understanding of the main activity.

Eid diary

RESOURCES

Per child, strip of plain paper, about 45cm x 15cm made into zigzag book; scissors; glue.

Activity Sheet 8 / 9

PERSONAL, SOCIAL AND EMOTIONAL DEVELOPMENT

Talk freely about their home and community. Have a sense of self as a member of different communities. Have a developing respect for their own cultures and beliefs and those of other people.

Key words

Eid, celebration, family, order

In this activity the children find out how a Muslim family celebrate their special day.

● Photocopy Activity Sheet 8 and cut out strips of plain paper, to fold to make zigzag books with four sections – one of each per child.

● Listen to 'Samira's Special Day'.

● Encourage the children to talk about the experiences and activities Samira describes. Invite the children to describe special family celebrations they might have. Sensitively discuss any similarities and differences.

● Give each child Activity Sheet 8 and a zigzag book. Encourage the children to talk about the pictures and the order in which they came in Samira's day. Ask the children to cut out the pictures then stick them in the right order in the zigzag book to make Samira's Eid diary.

Questions

What sort of things did Samira do at Eid?
Can you tell us about a family celebration you enjoy? What do you do?
What is happening in the pictures? Can you put them in the order Samira told us?

Eid Mubarak cards

RESOURCES

A4 card; scissors; coloured pencils; glue.

PHOTOCARD 4 / Activity Sheet 9

MATHEMATICAL DEVELOPMENT

Show an interest in shape and space by playing with shapes. Show an interest by talking about shapes. Begin to use mathematical names for flat 2D shapes and mathematical terms to describe shapes. Use language such as circle or bigger to describe the shape and size of flat shapes.

Key words

Shapes, sides, straight, curved, big, small, long, short, circle, semi-circle; square, oblong, triangle, crescent

20

Explore the properties of two-dimensional shapes by making Eid cards.

● Photocopy Activity Sheet 9 and fold A4 size card to make Eid cards – one of each per child – and give them out.

● Show the children Photocard 4. Encourage them to talk about the pictures and shapes they see.

● Ask the children to colour the shapes using colours they see in the pattern. Encourage them to talk about the shapes and introduce the key words into the discussion.

● Invite the children to cut out the shapes and arrange them on their card to make a picture or pattern. Encourage them to name the shapes and talk about which shapes fit together well and why.

● Suggest the children cut out the Eid Mubarak message and stick this inside the card.

Questions

What shapes and colours can you see on the Eid cards?
How can you fit your shapes together?
Which shapes fit together? Why?
Are there some shapes that don't fit together well? Why do you think that is?

Extension

Provide a selection of plastic 2D shapes. Encourage the children to create tessellating patterns, using ideas in the photocard to stimulate them.

Wall Poster

This giant poster can be used to introduce the topic of Celebrations and also provides a useful centrepiece for a display. The words to the songs, stories and poems on the CD are printed on the back of the poster and are accompanied by illustrations. Before putting up the poster, you may wish to enlarge the text on a photocopier for some of the children to follow as they listen to the CD. This will help the children begin to recognise words, even if they cannot 'read' the whole text. The words and illustrations can also be used as part of your display. You may wish to blank out the track numbers before photocopying the pages.

Photocards

The Photocards can often be used to start an activity and have been chosen to prompt discussion. The questions box offers suggestions of what to ask the children while you are using the Photocards. Try to work with a small group of children so that each picture can be seen clearly. You may also wish to start a collection, adding further photographs and magazine pictures from other sources.

Activity Sheets

Photocopiable Activity Sheets are provided to support particular activities. In some cases, the sheet may be used with a small group, while for other activities, each child will need their own copy. The Activity Sheets can be enlarged to A3, copied onto card and laminated so that they last longer. You might also wish to colour in the games.

CD

This CD will play on a CD player or computer with a CD drive and sound facility. Alternatively, you can copy the CD onto an audiotape if you do not have access to a CD player in your setting. The CD includes songs, rhymes, stories, poems and music – all of which are integrated into various activities. Each track is indicated by a numbered CD icon in the resources box. Transcripts of all CD tracks appear on the back of the Celebrations poster.

Planning chart

The planning chart below is to help you to plan your coverage of the Early Learning Goals and to enable you to match the activities to the children's ability level, indicated by the Stepping Stones. Each activity focuses on one main Early Learning Goal (indicated by a black circle in the planning chart) and may also cover secondary Early Learning Goals (indicated by a blank circle). There are two ways in which you may wish to use this chart:

- **Start with the Early Learning Goals and Stepping Stones**
  Decide which main Early Learning Goal you would like to cover and at what level (i.e. Stepping Stone). Use the planning chart below to choose an activity that meets your requirements. Refer to the activity page for a more detailed outline of the Stepping Stones covered by the activity. Ensure you keep a record of the Early Learning Goals and Stepping Stones you cover.

- **Start with the activities**
  From the chart below, choose an activity that is appropriate for your setting. Keep a record of the Early Learning Goals and Stepping Stones covered by the activity.

Early Learning Goals → / Stepping Stones →	Personal, social and emotional development				Communication, language and literacy				Mathematical development				Knowledge and understanding of the world				Physical development				Creative development			
	YELLOW	BLUE	GREEN	GREY	YELLOW	BLUE	GREEN	GREY	YELLOW	BLUE	GREEN	GREY	YELLOW	BLUE	GREEN	GREY	YELLOW	BLUE	GREEN	GREY	YELLOW	BLUE	GREEN	GREY
Happy New Year (p10)									●	●	●	●					○		○					
Dancing Dragons (p10)																	○	○	○	○	●	●	●	●
Rosh Hashanah Honey Sandwiches (p11)					●	●	●	●	○	○	○	○												
Flags for Sikh New Year (p11)													○	○	○	○	●		●	●				
Birthdays (p12)									○	○	○	○	●	●		●								
A New Arrival (p12)				●	○	○	○	○													○	○	○	○
Moving Day (p13)									●	●	●	●	○	○	○	○								○
We're planning a party! (p13)					●	●	●	●																
WEDDINGS																								
Tray for Muslim Sweets (p14)	○	○	○	○									●	●	●	●					○	○	○	○
Jewish Wedding Canopy (p14)	○	○	○	○	○	○	○	○									●		●		○	○	○	○
Decorated Hindu Hands (p15)																	○	○	○	○	●	●	●	●
Church Wedding (p15)	●	●			○	○	○	○						○	○									
Welcome Spring! (p16)						○							●	●		●								
May Day Mask (p16)													○	○		○					●	●	●	●

Early Learning Goals	Personal, social and emotional development	Communication, language and literacy	Mathematical development	Knowledge and understanding of the world	Physical development	Creative development
Sharing pancakes (p17)	● ● ●		○ ○ ○ ○			
Mardi Gras Parade (p17)					● ● ● ●	○ ○ ○ ○
Easter Crown (p18)			●　　●			○ ○ ○ ○
Easter egg hunt (p18)					● ●　●	
Hatching Easter chicks (p19)				● ● ● ●	○ ○ ○ ○	
Hot Cross buns (p19)		○　○	● ● ●			
Eid diary (p20)	● ● ●			○ ○ ○ ○		
Eid Mubarak cards (p20)	○ ○		● ● ● ●	○ ○		
Colours for Holi (p21)	○ ○			○ ○		● ● ● ●
Lotus garlands (p21)	● ● ● ●	○ ○				○ ○ ○ ○
Harvest colours (p22)				○ ○ ○ ○		● ● ● ●
Giving thanks (p22)	● ●	○　○				
A story for Purim (p23)		● ●　●				○ ○ ○ ○
Building a Sukkah (p23)				● ●　●	○　○	
DIVALI						
Diva lamps (p24)				○ ○	●　● ●	○ ○ ○ ○
Rama and Sita (p24)	● ● ● ●	○ ○　○				○ ○ ○ ○
Rangoli patterns (p25)				○ ○		● ● ● ●
A Story for Sikh Divali (p25)		●　●	○ ○ ○ ○	○ ○		
Fly Fish on Childrens' Day (p26)					○ ○ ○ ○	● ●　●
Halloween game (p26)	○ ○		● ● ● ●			
Sounds like Bonfire night! (p27)		● ●　●				○ ○ ○ ○
A window for All Saints (p27)				○ ○ ○ ○	○ ○ ○ ○	● ●　●
CHRISTMAS						
Gifts for Baby Jesus (p28)		●　●			○ ○ ○ ○	○ ○ ○ ○
Wrapping paper patterns (p28)			●			○ ○ ○ ○
Wrapping gifts (p29)	○ ○ ○ ○		● ● ● ●			○ ○ ○ ○
Postcard for Father Christmas (p29)	○ ○ ○ ○	●　● ●				○ ○ ○ ○

Happy New Year

MATHEMATICAL DEVELOPMENT

Show an interest in numbers and counting. Willingly attempt to count, with some numbers in the correct order. Count actions or objects that cannot be moved. Say and use the number names in order in familiar contexts.

Key words

first, second, third, number names, more, less, order

Invite the children to celebrate the New Year by completing this activity based on the Scottish first-footing custom.

● Photocopy Activity Sheet 1 on to card – one per child.

● Listen to the 'New things to do' song and encourage the children to talk about new places, people and things they would like to see and do.

● Explain that at New Year in Scotland it is lucky if the first person to come through the front door is carrying a piece of coal.

● Hand out the sheets and help the children to cut out their house. Ask them to choose one new thing they would like to do or see and draw this on a piece of paper. Help the children fold the sides of their houses so they are free-standing.

● Help the children cut open the door and tape their picture behind. When the door opens it reveals the new thing to do. Let the children write, or dictate, the significance of the picture behind the door.

Questions

In the new year what would you like to do?
Where would you like to go?
Who would you like to see? Why?
Which house is first ?
Which is second?

Extension

Help the children number their houses and stand them in numerical order. Encourage discussion about the numbers and ask them to identify the first, second, third house.

Dancing dragons

CREATIVE DEVELOPMENT

Show an interest in what they see, hear, touch, feel. Begin to use representation as a means of communication. Respond to comments and questions, entering into a dialogue about their creations. Express and communicate ideas, thoughts and feelings by using a widening range of materials.

Key words

dragon, mask, colour, shape, feel, move

Use Photocard 1 to inspire the children to make their own Chinese dragon masks and use them in a celebratory dance.

● Before the activity, cut out masks – oval shaped card with eyeholes – one per child.

● Show the children Photocard 1 and play the Chinese music. Ask the children to describe the dragon, talk about what they know about dragons and what they think dragons are like.

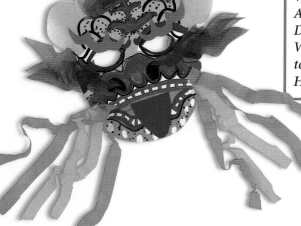

● Give each child a mask and encourage them to investigate the collage materials. Invite them to create their own dragon mask.

● Help the children staple coloured ribbon or crepe streamers to the sides of the mask and attach elastic.

● Listen to the Chinese music again. Encourage the children to respond to the music wearing their masks.

Questions

What colour is the dragon in the photo?
What do you know about dragons?
Are they real?
Do you know any stories about dragons?
What colours and materials will you choose to make your mask?
How do you move to the Chinese music?

Extension

Ask the children to describe their dragon. Is it a fierce or friendly dragon? What name could they give it? Ask them to make up an adventure for their dragon.

Honey sandwiches

RESOURCES

Bread; margarine; honey; apples; plates; safety knives; card for food labels (about 12cm square); selection of pens and pencils.

Knives must be safety knives

SAFETY

COMMUNICATION, LANGUAGE AND LITERACY

Sometimes give meaning to marks. Ascribe meanings to marks. Use writing as a means of recording and communicating. Write their own names and other things such as labels and captions.

Key words

name, label, word, write, letter, sound

Enjoy a celebratory meal of honey sandwiches to welcome the Jewish New Year (Rosh Hashanah).

● Give each child two slices of bread, margarine and honey. Help them make four honey sandwiches and put them on a plate.

● Help the children to cut half an apple into segments and put them on a plate.

● Invite them to lay the table for the meal.

● Give each child a piece of card folded to make a free-standing place name. Ask them to write their name on it, reinforcing the phonic values of letters written. Then ask which children would like to write labels for the plates of apples and sandwiches. Put the labels on the table.

● Ask the children to find their place names at the table and enjoy the meal!

Questions

What sound does 'apple' begin with? What sound does 'honey' begin with? What sound does your name begin with? Can you write your name and count the number of letters in it?

Extension

Give the children a range of writing materials and paper and ask them to write an invitation to the meal. Encourage them to illustrate it with drawings of apples, honey and bread.

Flags for Sikh New Year

RESOURCES

Per child, triangular yellow paper flag, length of crepe paper, art straw; stapler; glue; sticky tape.

PHYSICAL DEVELOPMENT

Encourage activities requiring hand-eye coordination. Manipulate materials to achieve a planned effect. Handle objects and construction materials safely and with increasing control.

Key words

triangle, wrap, wind, cover, attach

Celebrate the Sikh New Year (Baisakhi) by making simple, colourful flags.

● Before the session, cut out a yellow paper triangle and length of yellow crepe paper for each child.

● Explain to the children that Sikh New Year is celebrated by putting up a new yellow flag on a flagpole covered in yellow fabric.

● Give each child an art straw and help the children to tape the length of crepe paper to one end of the straw. Ask them to carefully wind the crepe paper around its length. Put sticky tape at intervals to ensure it stays attached to the flagpole.

● Let the children decide how to attach the triangular flag.

Questions

Can you find a way of wrapping the crepe paper around the art straw? How can you attach the flag? What are flags for?

Extension

Make more flags with yellow collage materials. Encourage the children to select, cut and stick their materials. Tell them yellow is an important colour for Sikhs and discuss their favourite colours.

Birthdays

RESOURCES

Children's own photographs taken at different ages; strips of paper; blu-tak

KNOWLEDGE AND UNDERSTANDING OF THE WORLD

Remember and talk about significant things that have happened to them. Begin to differentiate between past and present. Find out about past and present events in their own lives, and in those of their families and other people they know.

Key words

birthday, presents, older, younger, bigger, smaller, growing, change, difference, long ago, now

Use photographs of the children to help them see how they have changed over time.

● During the week before the activity, ask the children to bring in photographs taken at, or around, each of their birthdays, as well as of when they were born.

● Give each child a strip of paper and help them to arrange and stick down their photographs in chronological order.

● Encourage the children to talk about what they notice in each photograph, in particular how they have changed.

● Ask them what they think they might have been given for each birthday. Use this to stimulate talk about why a bike for a four-year-old would not be suitable for a one-year-old, for example.

Questions

Can you put your photos in the right order?
How are you changing as you grow older?
What can you do now that you couldn't do when you were one?
What were you given for your last birthday?
Would that have been a good present when you were one? Why/why not?

Extension

Make photocopies of the children's photos and help them to stick them on a strip of paper to make a time line. Invite them to draw a picture of a suitable birthday present.

A new arrival

RESOURCES

Collection of fiction and non-fiction books depicting new babies.

Activity Sheet 2

PERSONAL, SOCIAL AND EMOTIONAL DEVELOPMENT

Be sensitive to the needs of others.

Key words

clean, warm, fed, safe, clothes, blankets, presents

Use the matching game in this activity to start a discussion about the needs of a new baby.

● Photocopy Activity Sheet 2 on to A3 and cut out its ten component cards.

● Display some fiction and non-fiction books showing new babies in a variety of situations.

● Share the books with the children. Ask the children what is happening in the pictures. Ask them to talk about what a new baby needs e.g. to be fed, kept clean, warm and safe.

● Place the matching game cards face down. Invite up to five children to play the matching game. Ask one child to choose a picture, turn it over and describe it. Then ask the child to turn over other pictures until its partner is found.

● Encourage the child to explain why the pictures go together. Allow each child a turn.

Questions

What do we need to care for a new baby?
Why do the pictures go together?
What would make a good present for a new baby? Why?

Extension

Use the children's ideas to stimulate role play. Collect some of the following: clothes, towels, blankets, soft toys, and set up a water tray as a baby's bath. Invite the children to bring their 'gifts' and care for the baby.

Moving day!

RESOURCES

Large sheets of plain paper; model toys (buildings, fences, vehicles, people, etc); toy delivery van; thick marker pens.

PHOTOCARD **2**

MATHEMATICAL DEVELOPMENT

Show an interest in shape and space by making arrangements with objects. Show interest by talking about arrangements. Find items from positional or directional clues. Describe a simple journey. Use everyday words to describe position.

Key words

curved, straight, road, route, in front, behind, beside, left, right

---

Create a setting in which the children can help a delivery van find a new house and practise their positional language.

● Cover an area of the floor with large sheets of plain paper.

● Use model buildings, trees, play people, vehicles, etc, to lay out a town on the paper. The children can use thick pens to draw roads on the paper connecting the buildings.

● Show the children Photocard 2. Use this to stimulate talk about moving to a new home. Ask the children what sort of things the van might be carrying.

● Identify which building is to be the new house and give the children a toy delivery van which they can take turns to 'drive' to the new house. Encourage the children to describe their route using positional and mathematical language.

● Ask the children to draw a picture map of the scene to help visitors find the new house. Again encourage the use of positional language as they draw and when talking about their map.

Questions

Are the roads you have drawn straight or curved?
Can you describe where the new house is? What is in front? What is behind?
Can you describe the journey the delivery van takes?

Extension

Invite the children to take digital photos of the town scene from different positions. Use the photos to encourage spatial awareness and positional language. Ask the children to make some welcome banners. Display maps, digital photos, and banners alongside the photo of the delivery van.

We're planning a party!

RESOURCES

Large sheets of paper; large sheet of card; non-fiction books; coloured pencils and crayons.

COMMUNICATION, LANGUAGE AND LITERACY

Show interest in illustrations and print in books. Know information can be relayed in the form of print. Hold books the right way up and turn pages. Begin to recognise some familiar words. Know that print carries meaning and, in English, is read from left to right and top to bottom.

Key words

non-fiction book, word, information, contents, author, illustrator, letter

---

Plan and make a non-fiction big book about planning a party for all the family.

● Listen to the poem 'We're going to a party!' Then talk about what children do at a party and what they like doing best.

● Show the children a non-fiction book. Explain that it gives us information and the contents page tells us what we can read about.

Party-time

Authors Oliver Salazar, Ani Grimes, Torin Porter, Atula Nykiel, Gemma Knott, Rosa Milton, Alistair Noel, Thomas Ashman.
Illustrators George Scott, Kate Harris, Charlie Salazar, Mei Dadd, Sam Greshoff, Kamal Sayany, Jacob Hone.

● Ask the children to help make their own non-fiction book about things we need for a party. Invite them to suggest ideas for the contents page, such as food, music, games, things for mum, dad, grandparents etc.

● Write their ideas in large, clear print. Point out that you write from left to right and draw their attention to letter shapes and sound values. Number each idea. This will be the contents page.

● Ask the children to suggest ideas for each 'chapter' and ask them to illustrate their ideas.

● Once it is finished, put the sheets together and fold a large piece of card around them to make the front and back cover. On the front cover write the title, authors and illustrators.

Questions

What shall we list on our contents page?
Can you tell me your ideas?
Where do I need to start writing on the page? Which way do I go?

WEDDINGS

This group of activities highlights some similarities and differences between Muslim, Jewish, Hindu and Christian weddings.

Tray for Muslim sweets

KNOWLEDGE AND UNDERSTANDING OF THE WORLD

Express feelings about a significant personal event. Describe significant events for family and friends. Gain an awareness of the cultures and beliefs of others. Begin to know about their own cultures and beliefs and those of other people.

Key words

wedding, sweets, colour, pattern, clothes.

● Show the children the photograph of the Muslim wedding and ask them what they notice about the couple's clothes.

● Ask the children whether they have been to a wedding. If so ask them to talk about the clothes they and others wore and what they ate.

● Explain to the children that at a Muslim wedding the guests are given special sweets to eat. Invite them to make a tray for some wedding sweets.

● Give each child a paper plate and a selection of coloured pens and pencils.

● Draw their attention to the shapes, colours and patterns in the picture and encourage them to use these ideas in their drawings on the paper plate.

● Finally, encourage them to use modelling dough to make sweets and place them on their tray to offer to their friends.

Questions

What do you see in the picture?
What colours, shapes and patterns can you see?
What do you wear and what do you eat when you go to a wedding?

Jewish wedding canopy

PHYSICAL DEVELOPMENT

Construct with large materials such as long lengths of fabric and planks. Use a range of small and large equipment.

Key words

join, attach, build

● Show the children the photo of the Jewish wedding and ask them to describe the wedding canopy (huppah). Explain that it represents a house.

● Give the children a variety of large construction materials and encourage them to choose equipment to construct a house.

● Using a selection of home role-play resources, invite the children to develop their own home role-play.

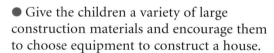

Questions

What do you think the wedding canopy is made from?
What equipment will you choose to build your house?
How can you join these things together?
How many children can fit in the house?

Decorated Hindu hands

CREATIVE DEVELOPMENT

Begin to differentiate colours. Differentiate marks and movements on paper. Make paintings and drawings. Explore colour, texture, shape, form and space in two dimensions.

Key words

fingers, hand, pattern, shape, colour, marks, prints

● Ask the children to describe the shape and colour of their hands.

● Show them the photo of the Hindu wedding and ask them to look carefully at the bride's patterned hands. Ask them to talk about the colours and shapes they see.

● Give each child a large sheet of plain paper and thin brown pens. Ask them to draw around their hands and then use the pens to fill their hand shapes with swirly patterns like the ones in the photo.

● Then give each child a thin paintbrush and a selection of ready-mixed paint. Encourage them to paint patterns on their hands and make hand prints.

● Ask the children to wash their hands and give them each a piece of rolled clay or modelling dough. Encourage them to make a hand print in this. Invite them to use simple clay tools and fingers to make marks and patterns in the print.

● Ask the children which of their designs they would choose for a wedding.

Questions

What colours, shapes and patterns can you see on the bride's hands?
What sort of shapes have you drawn on your hand outline?
What shapes and marks can you make in the clay/modelling dough?
Which of your hand patterns do you like best? Why?

Church wedding

PERSONAL, SOCIAL AND EMOTIONAL DEVELOPMENT

Show awareness of similarities in shapes in the environment. Begin to talk about the shapes of everyday objects. Begin to use mathematical names for solid 3D shapes and flat 2D shapes. Use language to describe the shape and size of solids and flat shapes.

Key words

box, cube, square, straight, edges, sides

● Photocopy Activity Sheet 3 – one per child.

● Point to the photo of the church wedding.

● Explain to the children that people celebrate by throwing coloured paper, called confetti, over the couple when they leave the church.

● Now ask the children to cut out the outline on the Activity Sheet. Help them to fold and stick the edges to make a simple cube box with an opening lid.

● Encourage them to cut, or tear, small pieces of tissue paper to fill their confetti box.

Questions

What can you see in the photograph?
Has your box got straight or curved edges?
What shape is each of the faces?
How many faces does your box have?
Can you see any other shapes like this?
Can you describe what you did to turn the flat shape into the box?

Welcome spring

RESOURCES

Activity Sheet 4

4-5

KNOWLEDGE AND UNDERSTANDING OF THE WORLD

Show an interest in the world in which they live. Comment and ask questions about where they live and the natural world. Observe, find out about and identify features in the place they live and the natural world.

Key words

spring, listen, sounds, changes, growing

Use this listening activity to discover how the world around us changes as we welcome the arrival of spring.

● Photocopy Activity Sheet 4 and give a copy to each child.

● Encourage the children to discuss what is happening in the pictures. Invite them to suggest at what time of year these events happen and where they might see them.

● Now listen to the song 'It happens each spring' and the spring sounds. Ask the children to listen carefully to the different

sounds. Suggest that they point to the corresponding picture on their sheet.

● Encourage them to talk about the things they like to do when the warmer weather and spring arrive.

Questions

What is going on in the pictures?
Where might you see these things?
What time of the year do you think we see these things? Why?
What sounds do these things make?
What do you like doing when the warmer weather comes?

Extension

Take the children on a walk locally to look for signs of spring. Bring some drawing paper and pencils and ask the children to sketch any new growth they see in the plants around them. Collect signs of new life to bring back. Make a display of the sketches and materials.

May Day mask

RESOURCES

Per child, paper plate; green, yellow, blue paint; paint brushes; water pots; mixing palettes; thin elastic; hole punch; scissors; coloured tissue paper; greenery; glue; stapler.

CREATIVE DEVELOPMENT

Begin to differentiate colours. Use their bodies to explore texture. Begin to describe the texture of things. Explore what happens when they mix colours. Make collages and paintings. Work creatively on a small scale. Explore colour, texture and shape in two or three dimensions.

Key words

greenery, yellow, blue, green, shade, shape, attach, leaves, branch, twig

Use two- and three-dimensional materials to create a mask of the traditional spring time figure of the Green Man.

● Before the activity, prepare a paper plate mask for each child, by cutting out holes for eyes and mouth.

● Take the children on a walk to collect pieces of greenery, such as leaves and grasses.

● On your return, give each child a paper plate. Invite them to cover this in green paint.

● Ask them to select some coloured pieces of tissue paper and scrunch them up to make flowers. Help them to attach these to the top of their masks to make the Green Man's crown.

● Then ask the children to choose some of the collected greenery to make the Green Man's beard. Help the children attach these to the bottom of the mask with glue or a stapler.

● When the masks are dry, attach elastic and let the Green Men parade to celebrate!

Questions

Can you describe how the grasses and leaves feel?
Can you describe the different shades of green you see?
Which colours and shapes make good flowers?
Which pieces of greenery make a good beard? Why?
How can you attach the flowers and beard to your mask?

Sharing pancakes

RESOURCES

Butter; milk; egg; large mixing bowl; whisk; frying pan; cooker; plates, safety knives, forks.

Keep children away from hot cooker.

Activity Sheet 5

SAFETY

PERSONAL, SOCIAL AND EMOTIONAL DEVELOPMENT

Demonstrate flexibility and adapt their behaviour to different events and social situations. Value and contribute to own well-being and self-control. Work as part of a group, taking turns and sharing fairly.

Key words

pancakes, mixing, sharing, turn-taking, fair, enough

Celebrate Shrove Tuesday by cooking pancakes in groups of 4 and encourage the children to share them fairly!

● Before the session, photocopy Activity Sheet 5 – one per group of 4.

● Group read the recipe together, drawing the children's attention to the print and any familiar words or letters.

● Follow the recipe sheet and encourage the children to take turns to mix the ingredients. Ask them why they think it is important to take turns.

● While you cook the pancakes, ask the children to listen to the song 'Mix a Pancake'.

● Now ask the children to lay enough places, plates and forks, for each child in the group.

● Then encourage the children to count the cooked pancakes. Encourage them to discuss how they could share them out among the group.

● Share out the pancakes in the way agreed by the group. If the pancakes do not share out equally, ask the children what they could do to make it fair. Now, enjoy the pancakes!

Questions

How do the ingredients change when we mix them together?
Why do we need to take turns?
How can we check that there is a place setting at the table for everyone?
What can we do to make sure everyone has the same number of pancakes?

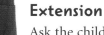

Extension

Ask the children to draw a sequence of pictures to show in what order the cooking events occurred. Encourage them to talk about what they did.

Mardi Gras parade

RESOURCES

Per child, 2 beaters.

PHOTOCARD 3

7

PHYSICAL DEVELOPMENT

Respond to rhythm and music by means of gesture and movement. Adjust speed to avoid obstacles. Initiate new combinations of movement and gesture in order to express and respond to ideas. Move with confidence, imagination and in safety.

Key words

parade, clap, beat, space, pathway

Use the carnival music in this activity to inspire controlled movement in an imaginative procession.

● Show the children Photocard 3 and encourage them to talk about what they see.

● Explain that in some countries people have carnivals in the streets.

● Ask the children to listen to 'Dis long time, gal' and to clap their hands in time to the music.

● Give each child a pair of beaters and ask them to stand in a line. Suggest that they imagine they are going to a Mardi Gras carnival.

● Encourage the children to move with the music, using their beaters to create their own Mardi Gras. Encourage them to use their space carefully and avoid bumping into others.

Questions

Can you describe what the people are doing in the photograph?
What would you most like to do in a parade?

Easter crowns

RESOURCES

Per child, pieces of card 50cm x 10cm; yellow tissue paper; brown paper; scissors; glue; stapler.

MATHEMATICAL DEVELOPMENT

Show an interest in shape and space by making arrangements with objects. Talk about, recognise and recreate patterns.

Key words

same, different, pattern, daffodil, crown

Help the children understand mathematical patterns by making an alternative to the traditional Easter bonnet.

● Before the session, cut out a length of card for each child.

● Invite the children to make daffodils by scrunching up small pieces of yellow tissue paper. Ask them to cut out small egg shapes from the brown paper.

● Demonstrate how to make a mathematical pattern by placing their completed eggs and daffodils in a pattern of daffodil, egg, daffodil, egg. Ask the children to clap the pattern they see by clapping hands, knees, hands, knees as they say the pattern.

● Invite the children to make their own pattern on their card by gluing or stapling the eggs and daffodils.

● Talk to the children about the patterns they have made. Staple the ends of the card to make Easter crowns.

Questions

Can you clap the mathematical pattern?

Extension

Invite the children to make small Easter nests by cutting out individual sections of egg boxes and painting them yellow or brown. When they are dry see if the children can arrange them in a colour pattern. Use them for an Easter display or in an Easter Egg Hunt.

Easter egg hunt

RESOURCES

A selection of outside play equipment, eg plastic tunnel, A-frame, tarpaulin, hoops, benches etc; small chocolate eggs — 1 per child.

PHYSICAL DEVELOPMENT

Manage body to create intended movements. Mount stairs, steps or climbing equipment using alternate feet. Travel around, under, over and through balancing and climbing equipment.

Key words

over, under, through, around, underneath, on top

This egg hunt encourages the children to develop their gross motor skills and also leads to a chocolate reward!

● Using a variety of outside play equipment, lay out a simple obstacle course. Ensure that there are obstacles for the children to travel over, under and through.

● At the end of the course place some simple Easter nests, each containing a small chocolate egg. Make sure there are enough for all the children.

● Invite the children to travel along the obstacle course and find an egg at the end.

Questions

How will you have to move to reach the Easter eggs?
Which of the obstacles will you have to travel over/under/through?
How did you have to move your body?
Which obstacles could you travel quickly over/through?

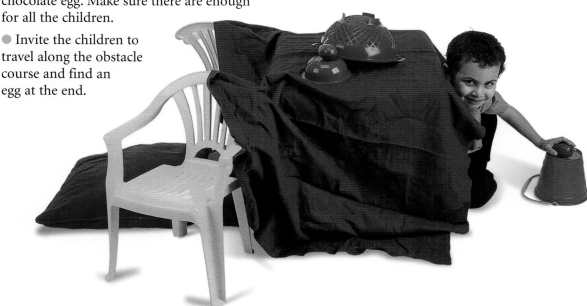

Hatching Easter chicks

RESOURCES

Scissors; staplers; hole punches; split pins; glue sticky tape.

Take care with split pins

 SAFETY

 Activity Sheet **6**

KNOWLEDGE AND UNDERSTANDING OF THE WORLD

Realise tools can be used for a purpose. Begin to try out a range of tools and techniques safely. Use simple tools and techniques competently and appropriately. Select the tools and techniques they need to assemble and join materials they are using.

Key words

tools, cut, join, fixed, movable

Help the children to practise simple cutting and joining techniques to make a hatching Easter chick.

● Photocopy Activity Sheet 6 on to card and give one to each child.

● Demonstrate how to use a hole punch, split pin and stapler.

● Give the children strips of card and paper and allow them time to explore and practise using the tools.

● Ask them to carefully cut out the shapes on the card, then arrange the three cut out shapes on the table to show the egg hatching.

● Encourage them to select appropriate tools and techniques to attach the chick to one half of the egg and to join the two egg halves so that it will open.

Questions

Which of these tools will make a hole?
How could you join two pieces of card?
Which of these tools will help you make a movable join?
How can you join the two halves of the egg so that they can open and close?

Hot cross buns

RESOURCES

Scissors; basket of penny coins; number line 0 to 5.

 Activity Sheet **7**

 8

MATHEMATICAL DEVELOPMENT

Show an interest in number problems. Sometimes show confidence and offer solutions to problems. In practical activities and discussion begin to use the vocabulary involved in subtracting. Begin to relate subtraction to taking away.

Key words

count back, take away, subtraction, more than, less than

Use this action song to encourage the children to relate taking away to subtraction.

● Photocopy Activity Sheet 7 onto A3 paper – one per child.

● Listen to the song 'Five Hot Cross Buns'. Use your fingers to represent each bun as it is being bought and encourage the children to do the same.

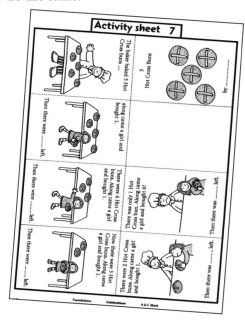

● Now ask five children to be the hot cross buns and to stand in a line. Sing the song again, with boys and girls taking it in turns to take a penny from the basket to buy a bun. As each child leaves the line, count the number left, emphasising that this number becomes smaller each time until there are none. Point to each numeral on a number line close by.

● Give each child Activity Sheet 7 and help them to cut and fold it into a book.

Questions

How many buns are there at the beginning of the song?
What happens to the number of buns as we buy them?
How many buns are left at the end of the song? Why?

Extension

Set up a baker's role-play area. Using shop role-play resources, suggest that the children buy buns and that they count how many buns are left after each purchase.

PERSONAL, SOCIAL AND EMOTIONAL DEVELOPMENT

Talk freely about their home and community. Have a sense of self as a member of different communities. Have a developing respect for their own cultures and beliefs and those of other people.

Key words

Eid, celebration, family, order

In this activity the children find out how a Muslim family celebrate their special day.

● Photocopy Activity Sheet 8 and cut out strips of plain paper, to fold to make zigzag books with four sections – one of each per child.

● Listen to 'Samira's Special Day'.

● Encourage the children to talk about the experiences and activities Samira describes. Invite the children to describe special family celebrations they might have. Sensitively discuss any similarities and differences.

● Give each child Activity Sheet 8 and a zigzag book. Encourage the children to talk about the pictures and the order in which they came in Samira's day. Ask the children to cut out the pictures then stick them in the right order in the zigzag book to make Samira's Eid diary.

Questions

What sort of things did Samira do at Eid? Can you tell us about a family celebration you enjoy? What do you do?
What is happening in the pictures? Can you put them in the order Samira told us?

MATHEMATICAL DEVELOPMENT

Show an interest in shape and space by playing with shapes. Show an interest by talking about shapes. Begin to use mathematical names for flat 2D shapes and mathematical terms to describe shapes. Use language such as circle or bigger to describe the shape and size of flat shapes.

Key words

Shapes, sides, straight, curved, big, small, long, short, circle, semi-circle; square, oblong, triangle, crescent

Explore the properties of two-dimensional shapes by making Eid cards.

● Photocopy Activity Sheet 9 and fold A4 size card to make Eid cards – one of each per child – and give them out.
● Show the children Photocard 4. Encourage them to talk about the pictures and shapes they see.
● Ask the children to colour the shapes using colours they see in the pattern. Encourage them to talk about the shapes and introduce the key words into the discussion.

● Invite the children to cut out the shapes and arrange them on their card to make a picture or pattern. Encourage them to name the shapes and talk about which shapes fit together well and why.
● Suggest the children cut out the Eid Mubarak message and stick this inside the card.

Questions

What shapes and colours can you see on the Eid cards?
How can you fit your shapes together?
Which shapes fit together? Why?
Are there some shapes that don't fit together well? Why do you think that is?

Extension

Provide a selection of plastic 2D shapes. Encourage the children to create tessellating patterns, using ideas in the photocard to stimulate them.

 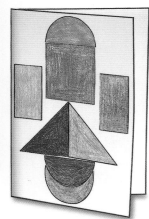

Colours for Holi

RESOURCES

Per child, paintbrush, painting apron, 2 pieces of paper; bowls of blue, green, yellow, red powder paint; jug of water.

CREATIVE DEVELOPMENT

Begin to differentiate colours. Differentiate marks on paper. Work creatively on a large or small scale. Explore colour in two dimensions.

Key words

paint, red, blue, yellow, green, mix, change, shape, pathway

Use the Hindu story in this activity to stimulate imaginative ways of painting.

- Listen to the story 'Krishna's Colours'.

- Show the children the bowls of powder paint. Ask them in turn to pour water into each bowl and stir with a paintbrush.

- Give them each a piece of paper and ask them to transfer paint from the bowls to their paper with a paintbrush.

- Then give each child a straw and encourage them to use this to blow the paint. Ask them what they notice about the pathways the blown paint makes.

- Now give them a new piece of paper and invite them to dip their brush into one of the paint bowls and to splatter paint across their paper. Encourage them to use different colours and ask them what happens to the colours when they merge.

- Ask the children to compare their paintings and to talk about the colours and shapes they have made.

Questions

How does the powder paint change when you add the water?
What happens to the paint when you blow it through your straw?
What shapes does the paint make on the paper?
What happens to the colours of the paint when it mixes with another?

Lotus garlands

RESOURCES

Scissors; thread; pink crayons

Activity Sheet
10

PERSONAL, SOCIAL AND EMOTIONAL DEVELOPMENT

Begin to accept the needs of others. Show care and concern for others. Have an awareness of the boundaries set and behavioural expectations within the setting. Consider the consequences of their words and actions for themselves and others.

Key words

help, care, share, thoughtful, kind, friendly

Use the garland making activity for the Buddhist festival of Wesak to stimulate discussion about caring for others.

- Photocopy Activity Sheet 10 – one per child.

- Help the children to cut out the lotus flower. Encourage them to shade the edge of each petal pink. Help them to roll up each petal to make them curl up slightly.

- Ask them to think about what they can do and say to others to show that they care. Encourage them to discuss their thoughts and introduce the key words.

- Now ask each child to choose some caring words and write one word clearly on each of their petals.

- Thread the lotus flowers together to make garlands. Display them around the room.

Questions

What do people say to you to make you happy?
What can you say to other people to make them happy?
How can you show other people you care for them?
What sort of things can you do to help other people?

Extension

Ask the children to make small baskets with modelling dough. Give them some pieces of white tissue paper and invite them to use this to make lotus flowers to fill their baskets.

Harvest colours

RESOURCES

Paper; harvest fruit and vegetables; magnifying hand lens; paintbrushes, powder/ready-mixed paint; mixing palettes; water pots, reproductions of still life paintings.

CREATIVE DEVELOPMENT

Begin to differentiate colours. Begin to describe the texture of things. Use lines to enclose a space, then begin to represent objects. Choose particular colours to use for a purpose. Make paintings and drawings. Explore colour, texture, shape form and space in two or three dimensions.

Key words

texture, feels like, colour, shade, mix

This activity helps children to develop painting techniques and skills by using the colour and textures of harvest produce as a stimulus.

● Show the children a selection of harvest fruit and vegetables, and ask them to feel the skins.

● Encourage them to use a hand lens to look at them closely.

● Ask the children to name the colours they see and describe the textures they feel.

● Then ask them to choose a piece of fruit or vegetable they would like to look at closely and paint. Encourage them to mix and apply paint to create an observational painting.

● Compare their paintings with reproductions of famous still life works.

Questions

Can you name the colours you see?
What do the fruit and vegetables feel like?
Can you describe their shapes?
Can you mix the paint on your palette to make the colours you see?
Can you paint the colours and shapes you see?

Extension

When the paintings are completed, encourage the children to discuss what they think about them. Ask them if they have been able to match the colours they see. Talk about the similarities and differences they notice between their paintings and the reproductions.

Giving thanks

RESOURCES

Per child, A4 size paper; pencils.

11

PERSONAL, SOCIAL AND EMOTIONAL DEVELOPMENT

Express needs and feelings on appropriate ways. Have a developing awareness of their own views and feelings.

Key words

Thanksgiving, thank you, pumpkin

Thanksgiving started in the early days of settlement in North America. Encourage the children to think about why and when they might be thankful.

● Before the session, cut out a pumpkin-shaped piece of paper for each child and give them out.

● Listen to the song 'Autumn Days'.

● Invite the children to discuss why and when they say 'thank you'.

● Ask the children to choose one thing they are thankful for. Write their thoughts in large clear print on their pumpkin.

● Share and discuss all the views and feelings written on the pumpkins.

Questions

Why do people say thank you?
When do you say thank you?
What sort of things can you say thank you for?

I am thankful for my family.

A story for Purim

RESOURCES

A selection of percussion instruments — 1 per child.

COMMUNICATION, LANGUAGE AND LITERACY

Listen to favourite stories. Join in with repeated refrains, anticipating key events and important phrases. Listen to stories with increasing attention and recall. Describe main story settings, events and principal characters. Sustain attentive listening, responding to what they have heard by relevant comments, questions or actions.

Key words

story, character, noise, instrument, sound, loud.

This activity encourages children to listen to a Jewish story and respond appropriately.

● Explain to the children that Jewish children listen to the story of Queen Esther at Purim. During the story when they hear the name of Haman they make lots of noise.

● Invite the children to choose a percussion instrument. Allow them time to explore the sound their instrument makes.

● Listen to the story 'Brave Queen Esther'. Encourage them to make as much noise as they can with their instruments when they hear Haman's name and to stop on a signal you give them.

● Encourage the children to talk about the story and what they thought about the main characters.

Questions

How can you use your instrument?
What sound does it make?
Do you think Queen Esther was good? Why?
What do you think of Haman?

Extension

Encourage the children to re-enact aspects of the story. Suggest that they use their instruments in their retelling.

Building a Sukkah

RESOURCES

Natural local materials; sticky tape; string; stapler.

PHOTOCARD
5

KNOWLEDGE AND UNDERSTANDING OF THE WORLD

Show an interest in the world in which they live. Comment and ask questions about the natural world. Observe, find out about and identify features in the natural world.

Key words

tree, hedge, bush, leaves, branch, stem

Celebrate the Jewish festival of Sukkot and investigate the natural world by building a shelter (sukkah).

● Show the children Photocard 5.

● Ask the children where they might be able to collect branches and leaves to make a roof like the one in the photograph.

● Go on a walk to collect leaves, fallen branches and other interesting natural things. Encourage them to talk about and describe what they see.

● On your return, ask the children to help you join the materials together. Drape them over chairs or large wooden blocks to make a simple sukkah.

Extension

Invite the children to make paper chains. Hang these in the sukkah to decorate it and suggest the children eat a celebratory snack inside.

Questions

What are the family doing in the picture?
What is their shelter like?
What materials is the roof made from?
Where do we find trees, hedges and bushes growing?

DIVALI

This group of four activities introduces the origins and some customs of the Hindu and Sikh light festival of Divali.

Diva lamp

RESOURCES

Per child — ball of clay, apron, night light; sequins.

SAFETY

Light the lamps away from the children

PHOTOCARD

6

PHYSICAL DEVELOPMENT

Engage in activities requiring hand-eye coordination. Explore malleable materials by patting, stroking, poking, squeezing, pinching and twisting them. Handle malleable materials safely and with increasing control.

Key words

Diva lamp, clay, fingers, thumbs, shapes, marks, push, pinch, squeeze, shapes, candle, light

● Show the children Photocard 6 and talk about what they see.

● Give each child a small piece of clay and ask them to make a pot. Encourage them to work the clay with their fingers and thumbs until the hole is large enough for a night light.

Questions

What do the diva lamps in the photograph look like?
How does the clay feel?
What shapes and marks can you make on the clay with your fingers and thumbs?
How can you make the hole big enough for a night light?
What shapes and patterns can you make on your diva with the sequins?

● Now give the children some sequins. Invite them to decorate the outside of their lamps by pushing them into the clay with their fingers.

● Ask the children to put a night light into their diva lamp. Carefully light the divas for them.

Rama and Sita

RESOURCES

Art straws; scissors; sticky tape; diva lamp.

Activity Sheet

11

13

PERSONAL, SOCIAL AND EMOTIONAL DEVELOPMENT

Begin to accept the needs of others, with support. Show care and concern for others. Have an awareness of the boundaries set and behavioural expectations within the setting. Understand what is right, what is wrong, and why.

Key words

good, helpful, kind

● Photocopy Activity Sheet 11 on to A3 card - one per child.

● Listen to the story 'Rama and Sita'.

● Ask the children to name the main characters and to describe events in the story.

● Give each child a copy of Activity Sheet 11. Help them to cut out the characters and attach each to an art straw. Let them use these to re-enact the story.

● Now ask the children to sit in a circle. Ask them to remember the good things that happened in the story. Then pass an unlit diva lamp around the circle, inviting each child who holds it to say something good they could do for others.

Questions

Who were the good characters in the story?
What did they do?
Who did the wrong things?
What good things can you do to help others?

Rangoli patterns

RESOURCES

Per child, 2 pieces of A4-sized black sugar paper; yellow and red tissue paper; glue; small bowls of red and yellow powder paint; small spoons.

CREATIVE DEVELOPMENT

Begin to differentiate colours. Use lines to enclose a space, then begin to use these shapes to represent objects. Explore what happens when they mix colours. Explore colour shape and space in two dimensions.

Key words

red, yellow, pattern, shape, Rangoli

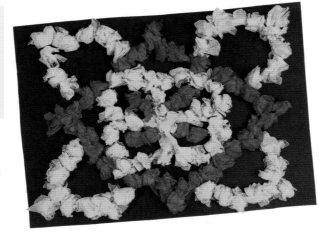

● Give each child two pieces of paper. Invite them to create a flower shape on one piece with scrunched up pieces of coloured tissue paper. Explain this is a sign of welcome.

● Now let each child choose a small bowl of dry powder paint. Invite them to make another Rangoli pattern on the second paper by using a spoon to sprinkle powder paint on their paper. Let them change colours when they wish. Talk to them about the shapes and colours they make.

● Ask them to compare the two patterns they have made. Encourage them to talk about which they like best and why.

Questions

How can you stick the tissue paper to make a flower shape?
What happens to the red and yellow powder paint when they mix on the paper?
Which of your patterns do you like best? Why?

Extension

Invite the children to use red and yellow chalk to make Rangoli patterns outside on the ground to welcome all those who arrive.

A story for Sikh Divali

RESOURCES

Per child, a strip of coloured paper about 20cm wide and of varying length (20cm to 100cm); plain paper (15x15cm); coloured pens; glue.

COMMUNICATION, LANGUAGE AND LITERACY

Listen to stories in small groups. Show an understanding of the main elements of stories, such as main character, sequence of events and openings.

Key words

character, guru, emperor, prince, prison, diva lamp, cloak, tassel, long, short, length

● Before the activity cut out strips of coloured paper, giving them each a tassel at one end – one per child.

● Listen to the story 'The Guru's Cloak'.

● Now give each child a paper tassel and a piece of plain paper.

● Ask them to talk about the main events in the story. Invite them to choose a character or event to draw on the paper, then stick this on their paper tassel.

Questions

Who were the special characters in the story?
What was special about the Guru's cloak?
Why did the people light diva lamps and candles?
Which part of the story would you like to draw? Why?
Who has the longest tassel and who has the shortest?

Extension

Ask the children to compare the lengths of their tassel paper. Encourage them to identify the longest and the shortest tassel, and to use mathematical vocabulary of length. Display the tassels in order of length.

Fly fish on Children's Day

CREATIVE DEVELOPMENT

Further explore an experience using a range of senses. Develop preferences for forms of expression. **Respond in a variety of ways to what they see, hear, touch and feel.**

Key words

twist, turn, run, jump, high, low, zigzag, spiral

Use a photograph of Japanese carp streamers to stimulate the children's creative responses in painting and movement.

● Give each child a crepe paper streamer.

● Show the children Photocard 7 and encourage them to describe the colours and designs they see.

● Invite the children to paint a fish along the length of their streamer.

● When the paint is dry, ask the children to take their streamers outside. Ask them to hold them up in the air and watch how they move in the breeze.

● Now introduce the key words and ask the children to move with their streamers in the way each word suggests. Encourage them to notice the shapes their streamers make, and to respond to this with their movement.

Questions

What colour will your fish be?
How does your streamer move in the breeze?
How does your body move with the streamer?

Extension

Invite the children to work in a group to paint a fish on a large piece of cotton or calico fabric. Make this into a flag and display it outside where the children can watch and talk about the movements it makes.

Halloween game

MATHEMATICAL DEVELOPMENT

Show an interest in numbers and counting. Willingly attempt to count, with some numbers in the correct order. Recognise numerals 1 to 5, then 1 to 9. Say the number name after any number up to 9. Count reliably up to 10 objects. Recognise numerals 1 to 9. Use developing mathematical ideas and methods to solve problems.

Key words

Count, number, more than, less than, count on, count back, first, second, third, fourth, number names to 12.

Practise counting and other maths skills with the Halloween board game.

● Photocopy Activity Sheet 12 on to A3.

● Listen to the 'This is Halloween' poem and encourage the children to talk about the activities it describes.

● Invite four children to play the board game and give each one a counter. Explain that they will need to take turns to throw the dice and count the number of spots shown when it lands. This will tell them how many steps to travel along the path.

● As the children play the game, introduce the key words where appropriate. Encourage them to count the dice spots accurately, to read the numeral they land on, and to count on and back where necessary.

● Use the words first, second, third and fourth as the children finish.

Questions

How many spots does the dice show?
How many places will you have to move?
What number did you land on?
Are you counting on or back along the path?
Are the numbers getting bigger or smaller?

Extension

Invite the children to make hats or masks depicting characters in the poem.

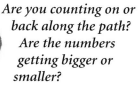

Bonfire night

Encourage the children to explore and experiment with letter sounds and descriptive words by listening to bonfires and fireworks.

● Begin by asking the children to listen to the track 'Bonfire night'.

● Encourage the children to think of words to describe the sounds they have heard. Introduce the key words and encourage them to use these, along with other words they might suggest, in their descriptions.

● Write the words they suggest clearly on a big board for them to see. Emphasise the initial sound of each word as you write.

Questions

Can you think of words to describe how the fireworks sound?
What words could you use to describe the noises a bonfire makes?
Can you make up your own words to describe the sounds you heard?

RESOURCES
Large paper; pen

16

COMMUNICATION, LANGUAGE AND LITERACY

Show an interest in print in the environment. Understand the concept of a word. Explore and experiment with sounds and words.

Key words
bang, pop, crackle, sizzle, whoosh, whizz, fizz

Extension
Encourage the children to work as a group to paint a large rocket. Make its explosive tail from strips of paper and help the children to write descriptive words on it. Display it under the title 'Bonfire night sounds like…'

A window for All Saints

Inspire the children to make a stained-glass window for this Christian festival.

● Show the children Photocard 8 and ask them to describe what they see. Explain the significance of the saints and ask the children who is special to them.

● Give each child a piece of black sugar paper. Invite them to design and make a window for their special person. Help them to cut out shapes and stick tissue paper or cellophane behind.

● On a slip of paper write the child's name and the name of their special person. Ask the children to stick this at the top.

● Finally, ask the children to hold their windows up to the light and ask them to talk about what they notice.

Questions

Who is special to you?
What colours do you think they like?
What shapes and colours will you use?
What do you notice when you hold it up to the light?

RESOURCES
Per child, A4-size black sugar paper, slip of paper; coloured tissue paper; coloured cellophane; scissors; glue; sticky tape.

PHOTOCARD

8

CREATIVE DEVELOPMENT
Begin to use representation as a means of communication. Talk about personal intentions, describing what they were trying to do. Express and communicate their ideas, thoughts and feelings by using a widening range of materials and tools, and designing and making.

Key words
Saint, special, colours, shapes, stained glass, light.

Rory's special person is James

Extension
Fill a play tray with a selection of transparent materials, such as tissue paper, cellophane, coloured plastics, etc, and provide a torch. Invite the children to explore the materials by holding them up to a light source. Ask them what they notice and which materials let the light through most easily.

CHRISTMAS

Explore the significance of giving presents at Christmas through these four mathematical and language-based activities.

Gift for baby Jesus

RESOURCES

scissors.

COMMUNICATION, LANGUAGE AND LITERACY

Listen to stories with increasing attention and recall. Describe main story settings, events, and principal characters. Listen with enjoyment, and respond to stories and poems and make up their own stories, songs, rhymes and poems.

Key words

presents, gifts, Kings, Jesus, Mary, Joseph, shepherds, characters

● Photocopy Activity Sheet 13 on to card - one per child – and give out.

● Begin the session by listening to the poem 'The Riding Kings'.

● Ask the children to talk about the main characters in the poem and what they were doing. Discuss with them the role of the kings in the Christmas story.

● Now ask the children to cut out the figures and to fold back the tabs so they are free standing.

● Encourage the children to use the figures in role-play retelling the Christmas story and to develop their own ideas.

Questions

Who brought presents in the poem?
Why do you think they brought presents?
Who else brought presents in the story?
Can you use your characters to tell a Christmas story?

Extension

Invite the children to fill a piece of A4-size card with a drawing of a stable. Help them to cut and fold back the sides to make it free standing. Then help them to paper clip the characters on to the card to make a nativity scene to display.

Wrapping paper patterns

RESOURCES

Per group of 6, 6 pieces of newsprint paper, 6 potato prints, 3 bowls of green ready-mixed paint and 3 bowls of red; selection of wrapping paper with repeated patterns.

MATHEMATICAL DEVELOPMENT

Talk about, recognise and recreate simple patterns.

Key words

same, different, pattern, repeat, colour, shape

● Beforehand, collect sheets of wrapping paper with repeating patterns. Cut three potatoes in half and cut a Christmas tree shape out of each half.

● Begin the activity by showing the children the wrapping paper and drawing their attention to the repeated patterns.

● Give each child a sheet of newsprint. Ask them to make their own repeating pattern using the potato prints with green and red paint. Encourage them to fill the paper with lines of patterns.

Questions

Which shapes and colours are the same and which are different on the wrapping paper?
What pattern can you make?
Can you change your pattern? How?

Extension

Cut out more Christmas shapes from potatoes and invite the children to extend their pattern-making by alternating different shapes as well as colours to make more wrapping paper. When it is dry, use it in the 'Wrapping Gifts' activity.

Wrapping gifts

RESOURCES

A selection of boxes and packaging; Christmas wrapping paper; sticky tape.

MATHEMATICAL DEVELOPMENT

Show an awareness of similarities in shapes in the environment. Use language such as 'big' and 'little'. Show an interest by talking about shapes. Begin to use mathematical names for 'solid' 3D shapes and 'flat' 2D shapes and mathematical terms to describe shapes. Use language such as 'circle' or 'bigger' to describe the shape and size of solid and flat shapes.

Key words

long, short, curved, straight, sides, edges, faces, circle, square, oblong, cube, cuboid, cylinder, cone

● Before the activity, collect a variety of packaging and boxes, ensuring that you have some cylinders, cubes, cuboids and cones, and enough for one per child.

● Begin by showing the children the boxes and asking them what they notice about the shapes. Introduce the key words into your discussion and encourage them to use some of these words in their descriptions.

● Now give the children some wrapping paper and ask them to select a box to wrap. Encourage them to lie the paper flat against each face of their box, drawing their attention to the shape's properties and key words. Help them to use sticky tape to secure the paper.

Questions

Which are the biggest and which are the smallest shapes?
Which shapes have straight edges and which have curved ones?
Which words can you use to describe these shapes?
What present would fit into your package?

Extension

Set up a Post Office role-play area. Include four post sacks labelled clearly with the written word and picture of cubes, cuboids, cylinders and cones. Encourage the children to sort the wrapped parcels in their play.

Postcard for Father Christmas

RESOURCES

Pencils; coloured pencils; glue

Activity Sheet

14

COMMUNICATION, LANGUAGE AND LITERACY

Distinguish one sound from another. Hear and say initial sound in words and know which letters represent some of the sounds. Link sounds to letters, naming and sounding the letters of the alphabet. Write simple words and make phonetically plausible attempts at more complex words.

Key words

postcard, letter sound, address, stamp

● Photocopy Activity Sheet 14 and give out – one per child.

● Help the children to fold and stick the paper to make a postcard.

● Invite them to write their postcards to Father Christmas asking for the presents they would like.

● Encourage them to attempt their own writing, drawing their attention to letter sounds and the letters they represent.

● Now ask the children to design and draw their own stamp in the space and a picture of themselves opening their present on the front.

Questions

What would you like for Christmas?
What sound does it begin with?
What letter makes that sound?
What other sounds can you hear in that word?
How many different letters have you written?

Extension

Talk to the children about addresses. Help them to address their postcards to Father Christmas. Use some of the postcards in the Post Office role-play.

Display ideas

Displays can be used to stimulate interest in a topic or to reinforce an idea or skill. Displaying children's work can add value to what they have done, raise self-esteem and help them learn to share. Good displays can lead to a stimulating environment and give great pleasure, both to the children who create the displays and to their parents and carers who come to admire them. The following display suggestions make use of the activities and resources in this pack.

Display tips
● Wallpapers make long-lasting backgrounds that do not fade as quickly as sugar papers.
● Newspaper makes an interesting background for buildings and brick effects.
● Corrugated card helps to provide 3-D parts for flat displays. It is particularly useful for trees and logs.
● Borders around displays help to focus eyes on the display contents.
● Ceilings, cupboards and windows are valuable display areas.

Happy New Year (see page 10)

● Cover a table in grey paper and draw a road along its length.

● Invite the children to paint a street scene and attach this behind the table.

● Stand the children's houses in numerical order along the road. Write a label 'New Street' and attach this to the first house.

● Display labels alongside.
'Come and find out what we would like to do in the New Year!'
'What is in number 1?' etc

● Put play people and toy vehicles along the street to enable the children to 'visit' each house and encourage interaction with the display.

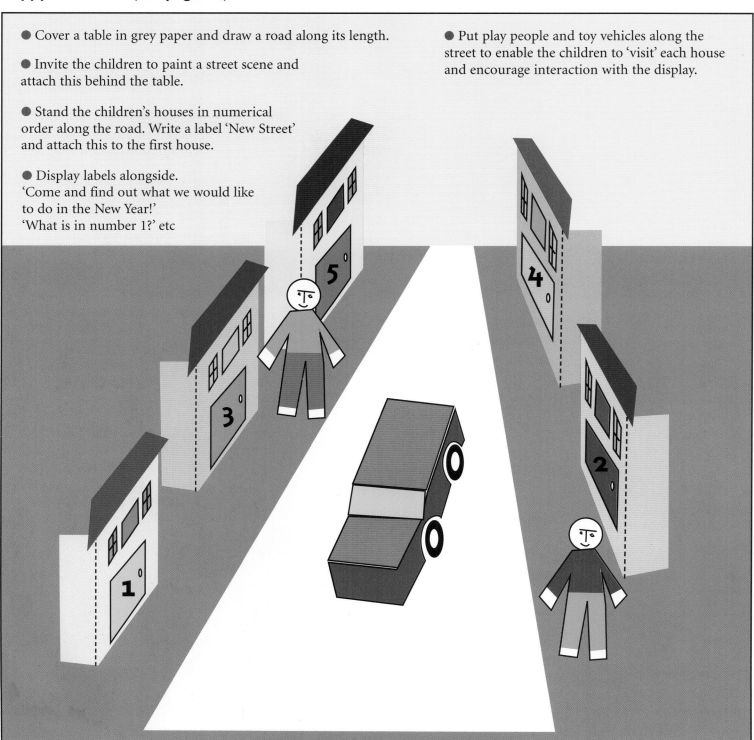

Eid Mubarak Cards (see page 20)

● Cover a display board with red backing paper.

● Arrange and pin on the children's Eid cards. Cut out crescent shapes from silver paper and intermingle these with the children's work. Display Photocard 4 alongside

● In front of the display board, cover a table in black sugar paper. On a strip of white paper write the questions 'What other Eid patterns can you make?' 'What shapes will you use?' Stick this at the top of the table.

● Cut out of thick card a selection of large 2D shapes and cover them in silver paper

● Place these on the table and encourage the children to play with the shapes and make new designs

Harvest colours (see page 22)

● Cover a display board in neutral backing paper. Double mount children's paintings, arrange and pin on the board.

● In front of the board, cover a table with a green cloth.

● Put a selection of harvest fruit and vegetables into a basket and place on the table. Put some magnifying hand lenses beside them.

● Place a selection of art books and reproductions of still life on the table.

● Encourage the children to use the hand lenses to observe the fruit and vegetables and to look at the art books.

Wrapping gifts (see page 29)

● Cut out the shapes of four post vans. Invite the children to paint them red with a driver inside.

● Cover a display board with grey paper and paint on road markings. Use white paint or spray snow to look like snow on the road.

● Position and attach the vans along the road.

● Label each van clearly with a sign, and corresponding drawing, saying:
The parcels in this van are cylinders
The parcels in this van are cubes
The parcels in this van are cones
The parcels in this van are cuboids

● Cut out four large pieces of silver paper to represent a window and attach one to each van.

● Attach some wrapped parcels on top of the window of the corresponding van.

THE PARCELS IN THIS VAN ARE CUBES

Festival calendar

Hogmanay

DATE: 31 DECEMBER

PLACE: SCOTLAND

This festival celebrates the end of the old year and the beginning of the new. Sometimes a blazing tar barrel is rolled down the street. People go 'first-footing', bringing good luck by being the first person to enter someone's home carrying a piece of coal.

Chinese New Year (Yuan Tan)

DATE: BETWEEN 17 JANUARY-19 FEBRUARY

PLACE: CHINA AND CHINESE COMMUNITIES

Chinese celebrate the new year by cleaning their houses to sweep out the old, ready to welcome the new. They believe evil spirits are around at new year, so to keep them away they light firecrackers. Street processions led by huge paper dragons welcome the new year.

Shrove Tuesday (Pancake Day)

DATE: FEBRUARY/MARCH

(LAST DAY BEFORE LENT)

RELIGION: CHRISTIAN

Christians give up eating certain foods to remind themselves of Christ's fasting in the wilderness for 40 days and nights. Pancakes are cooked as a way of using up rich foods before the period of Lent.

Mardi Gras

DATE: FEBRUARY/MARCH

(LAST DAY BEFORE LENT)

RELIGION: CHRISTIAN

People celebrate the last day of eating well before Lent by taking to the streets in processions particularly in New Orleans, Trinidad and Rio de Janeiro. There are huge carnivals with music, dancing and costumes.

Purim

DATE: FEBRUARY/MARCH

RELIGION: JEWISH

This festival commemorates Queen Esther who saved the Jews from slaughter. Children re-enact her story, booing and shouting when the name of the wicked Haman is said. People enjoy a celebratory meal and sweets and fruit are given.

Saint David's Day

DATE: 1 MARCH

PLACE: WALES

Patron saint of Wales. People often wear symbols of Wales, such as a daffodil. Musical concerts are often held in celebration.

Saint Patrick's Day

DATE: 17 MARCH

PLACE: IRELAND

Patron saint of Ireland. He is remembered for his life of prayer and for establishing religious houses for monks and nuns. People celebrate by praying and wearing a shamrock.

Mother's Day

DATE: MARCH

RELIGION: CHRISTIAN

This celebration grew out of 'Mothering Sunday' when Christians visited their local, or 'mother', church. Today children celebrate by giving their mothers cards and flowers in recognition of the care and love they give. It is celebrated on the fourth Sunday in Lent.

Pessach (Passover)

DATE: MARCH/APRIL

RELIGION: JEWISH

This festival commemorates the release of the Jews from slavery by Moses and the passage into 'the promised land'. Celebrations last for eight days and celebratory meals are enjoyed, the main one being Seder.

Holi

DATE: MARCH/APRIL

RELIGION: HINDU

This festival celebrates new life and the triumph of good over evil. Traditional stories are told about Krishna and Prahlad. People light bonfires and throw coloured water and dyes over one another.

Easter

DATE: MARCH/APRIL

RELIGION: CHRISTIAN

The most important spiritual festival in the Christian year. It celebrates the joy of Jesus' resurrection after his crucifixion on Good Friday. Painted or chocolate eggs are given to represent new life.

Baisakhi

DATE: 13 APRIL

RELIGION: SIKH

This festival celebrates the Sikh new year and the birthday of Khalsa (community of initiated Sikhs). The flagpole outside the gurdwara is taken down, its fabric wrapping (chola) removed. It is given a new chola and flag, and is raised to celebrate the new year.

Saint George's Day

DATE: 23 APRIL

PLACE: ENGLAND

Patron saint of England, who is remembered for killing a dragon and encouraging people to be baptised. Some people wear a rose when they celebrate the day and churches raise St George's flag.

May Day

DATE: 1 MAY

PLACE: NORTHERN EUROPE

Traditionally celebrated by dancing around a maypole, which was believed to encourage the crops to grow. Often green leaves were worn in hats, modelled on the pagan Green Man. He was a symbol who represented links between the people and the earth.

Kodomono-Hi (Children's Day)

DATE: 5 MAY

PLACE: JAPAN

Originally Boys' Day, this festival is celebrated by flying kites, or streamers in the shape of carp. The carp represent the strength and courage the boys will need in life.

Wesak

DATE: MAY

PLACE: BUDDHIST

This, the most important Buddhist festival, takes place at a time of full moon. It celebrates Buddha's birth, enlightenment and death. Lotus flowers are displayed in homes, in baskets and garlands.

Raksha Bandhan

DATE: JULY/AUGUST

RELIGION: HINDU

This family festival celebrates the relationship between brothers and sisters. Sisters tie a bracelet (rakhi) around their brothers' wrist to bring them good luck. In return, the brothers promise to protect their sisters.

Lantern Festival

DATE: AUGUST

PLACE: JAPAN

To celebrate the ripening of the rice, the Japanese take to the streets in a procession. They carry an array of large colourful paper lanterns. Each lantern represents a single grain of rice.

Janmashtami

DATE: AUGUST/SEPTEMBER

RELIGION: HINDU

A celebration of Krishna's birth. At midnight temple bells ring and a statue of Krishna is placed in a cradle. Stories of Krishna are told and boys enact a favourite story by stealing butter and rice from high windows.

Rosh Hashanah

DATE: SEPTEMBER/OCTOBER

RELIGION: JEWISH

It marks the beginning of the Jewish new year and the ten Holy Days (penitence). Families eat special meals, the first of which includes slices of apple and bread dipped in honey, to wish them a 'sweet new year'.

Yom Kippur

DATE: SEPTEMBER/OCTOBER

RELIGION: JEWISH

This is the holiest and the last of the ten days of Penitence. People go without food on the day itself. Prayers for forgiveness are said in the synagogue and the day ends with the blowing of a horn (shofar). People then go home for a special meal.

Sukkot

DATE: SEPTEMBER/OCTOBER

RELIGION: JEWISH

This week-long festival celebrates the time when the Jews travelled from Egypt to Israel. Families build a three-sided shelter (sukkah) with rows of leaves and branches. They are decorated with citrus fruits and paper chains. Families eat their meals here to remind themselves of their ancestors.

Harvest Festival

DATE: SEPTEMBER/OCTOBER

RELIGION: CHRISTIAN

Christians celebrate the safe gathering in of the harvest. The church is decorated with flowers and harvest produce. A service of thanks is given and some churches hold a special harvest supper.

Halloween

DATE: 31 OCTOBER

PLACE: PARTS OF THE BRITISH ISLES, USA

Traditionally, it was believed that at this festival, held on All Saints eve, ghosts came to haunt. Bonfires and lanterns were lit to keep ghosts and witches away. Today, children dress up as witches and ghosts and play 'trick or treat'. This game is based on the belief that if the spirits were kept happy they would leave people alone. If not, they would play tricks.

Divali

DATE: OCTOBER/NOVEMBER

RELIGION: HINDU AND SIKH

For Hindus, this festival of light marks the beginning of their new year and the triumph of good over evil. Diva lamps are lit in remembrance of the safe return of Rama and Sita, and rangoli patterns are made on the floor. Although the Sikh community celebrate in the same way, they remember the release of Guru Hargobind from prison.

All Saints

DATE: 1 NOVEMBER

RELIGION: CHRISTIAN

This is a celebration of the lives and good works of all the saints. Many Christians go to church to give thanks for the good examples of faith and a model for Christian life that they have set.

Bonfire Night

DATE: 5 NOVEMBER

PLACE: BRITAIN

This festival reminds people about the unsuccessful attempt by Guy Fawkes to blow up the Houses of Parliament in 1605. He was captured and hung for treason. Fireworks are lit and bonfires often burn models of Guy Fawkes.

Thanksgiving

DATE: FOURTH THURSDAY OF NOVEMBER

PLACE: USA

This celebration commemorates the first harvest of the English settlers in 1621. Today, it is held when the harvest is safely gathered and families share a special meal of turkey, followed by pumpkin pie. They give thanks for all the good things of the past year.

St Andrew's Day

DATE: 30 NOVEMBER

PLACE: SCOTLAND

Patron saint of Scotland, whom the Anglican Church recognises as one of the first missionaries. People celebrate this day with prayer and remember those agencies, and individuals committed to missionary work.

Hanukkah

DATE: NOVEMBER/DECEMBER

RELIGION: JEWISH

This eight-day festival of light celebrates the time when the Jews won back their temple from the Greeks. They found a lamp with one day's worth of oil which miraculously stayed alight for eight days. Today, Jews light one candle on the first night, two on the second and so on, using a special candlestick.

Saint Nicholas' Day

DATE: 6 DECEMBER

RELIGION: CHRISTIAN

This festival celebrates the birth of the patron saint of children. He was said to visit European children on the eve of his birthday. In Holland he was known as Sinter Klaas and he is the figure upon whom Father Christmas is based.

Christmas

DATE: 25 DECEMBER

RELIGION: CHRISTIAN

This festival celebrates of the birth of Christ. Christians worship in church, sing carols and give and receive presents. Children believe Father Christmas brings presents while they sleep on Christmas Eve.

Moveable Islamic Celebrations

The Muslim calendar has 12 months, each starting with a new moon. This means that months are either 29 or 30 days long. There are six annual celebrations, including two big festivals.

Eid-ul-Fitr

This is one of the big festivals and it occurs at the end of Ramadan. During the holy month of Ramadan, Muslims fast between sunrise and sunset. The fast is broken by Eid celebrations, that consist of prayers of thanks, celebratory meals, and the exchange of cards and presents.

Eid-ul-Adha

The second festival commemorates the time when Abraham decided to sacrifice his son to Allah, and how Allah put a ram in his place. Muslims eat a special meal of roast lamb and hope to visit Mecca for this festival at least once during their lifetime.

Muharram

Muslim new year, or Muharram, is a time for Muslims to reflect on how to live their lives closer to Islam. There are no parties or big celebrations, merely an exchange of new year greetings and spiritual discussion.

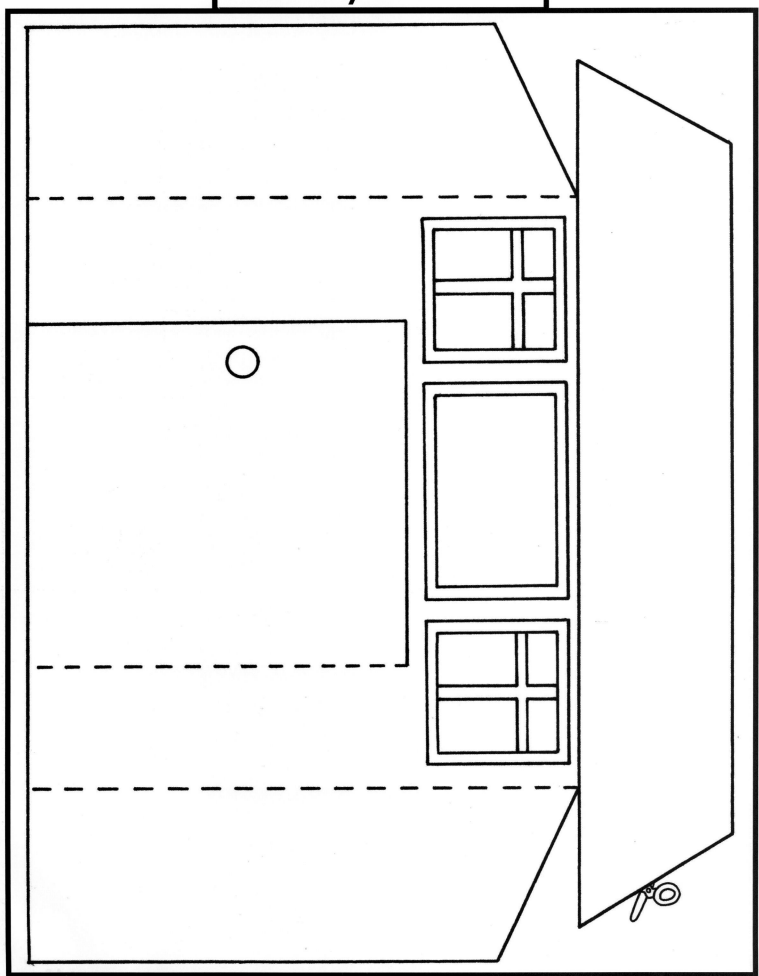

Foundations   **Celebrations**   A & C Black

Activity sheet 2

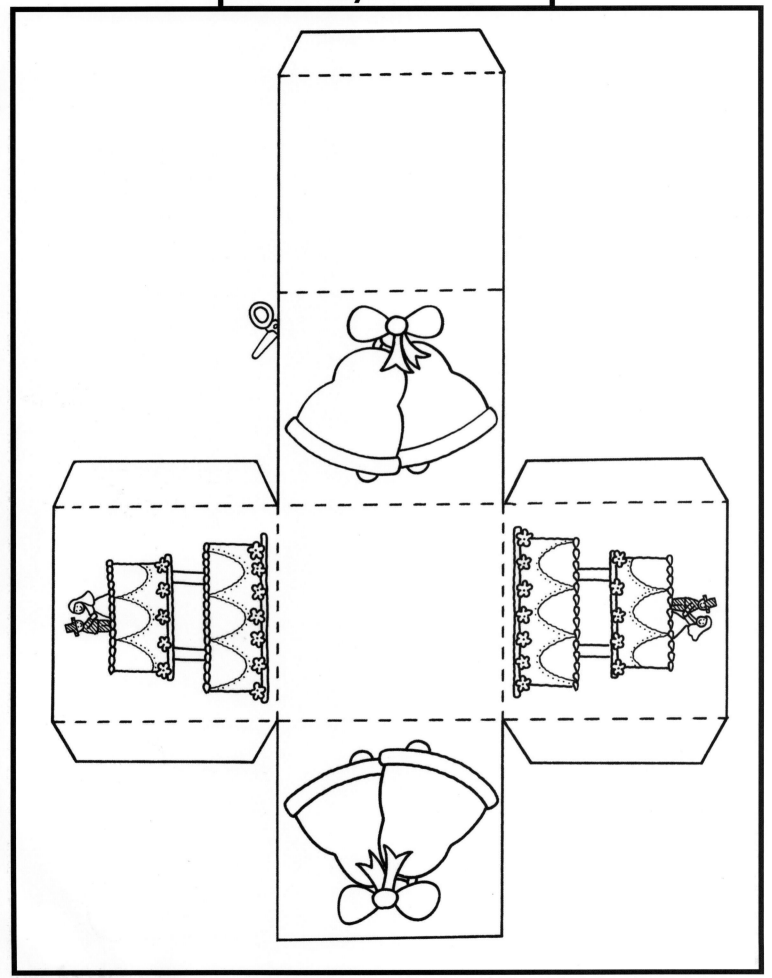

Foundations   **Celebrations**   A & C Black

PANCAKE RECIPE

Ingredients

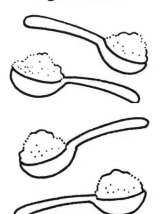

4 tablespoons
of plain flour

1 cup of milk

1 egg

1 piece of butter

Instructions

1. Put the flour into the bowl.

2. Break the egg
into the bowl.

3. Add the milk.

4. Whisk the ingredients
until they form a batter.

5. Ask an adult to melt the butter
in a frying pan and cook the
pancake.

5
Hot Cross Buns

by ....

The baker baked 5 Hot Cross buns ....

along came a girl and bought 1.

Then there were .... left.

There were 4 Hot Cross buns. Along came a girl and bought 1.

Then there were .... left.

There was only 1 Hot Cross bun. Along came a girl and bought it!

Then there was .... left.

Now there were 3 Hot Cross buns. Along came a girl and bought 1.

Then there were .... left.

There were 2 Hot Cross buns. Along came a girl and bought 1.

Then there was .... left.

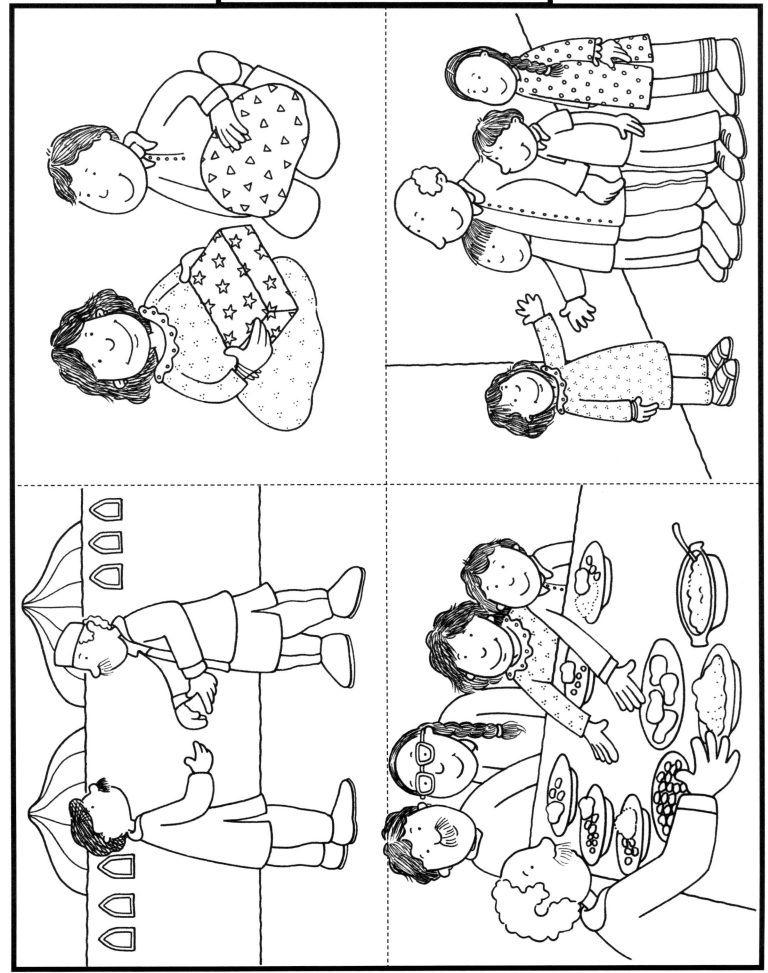

Foundations   **Celebrations**   A & C Black

Activity sheet 11

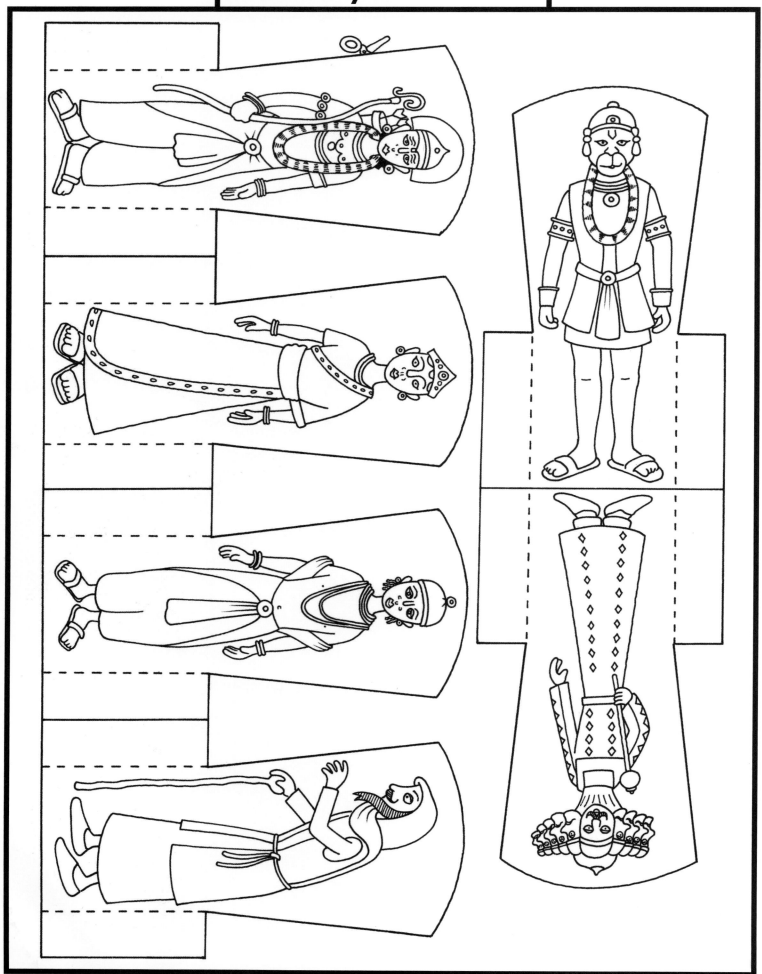

Foundations **Celebrations** A & C Black

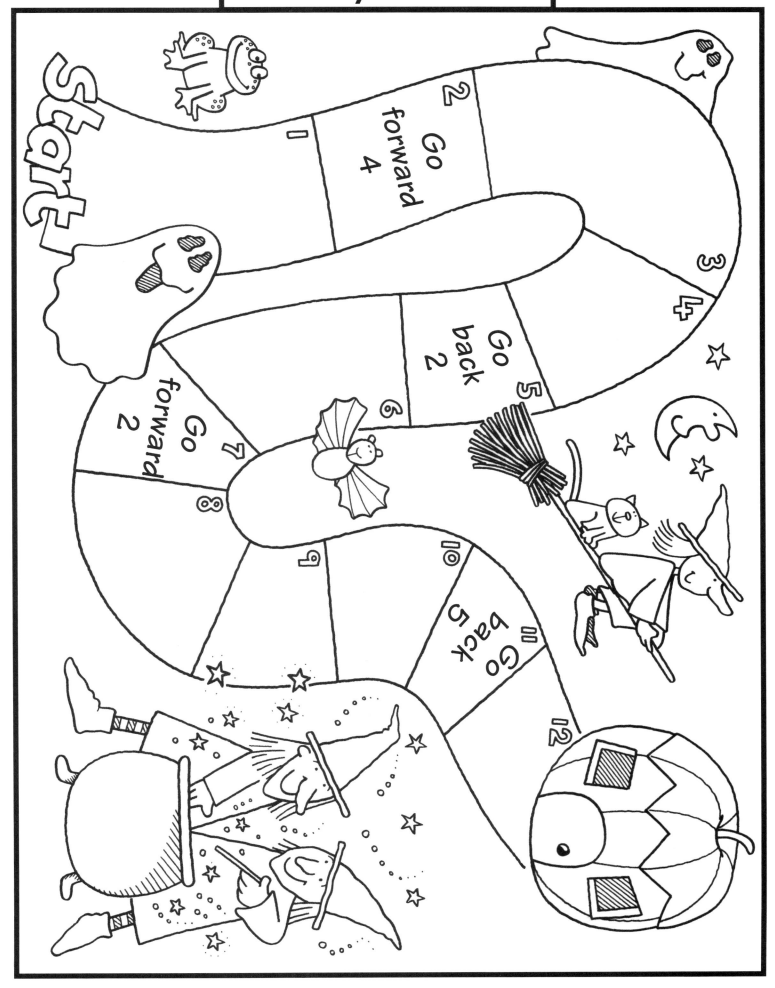

Activity sheet 13

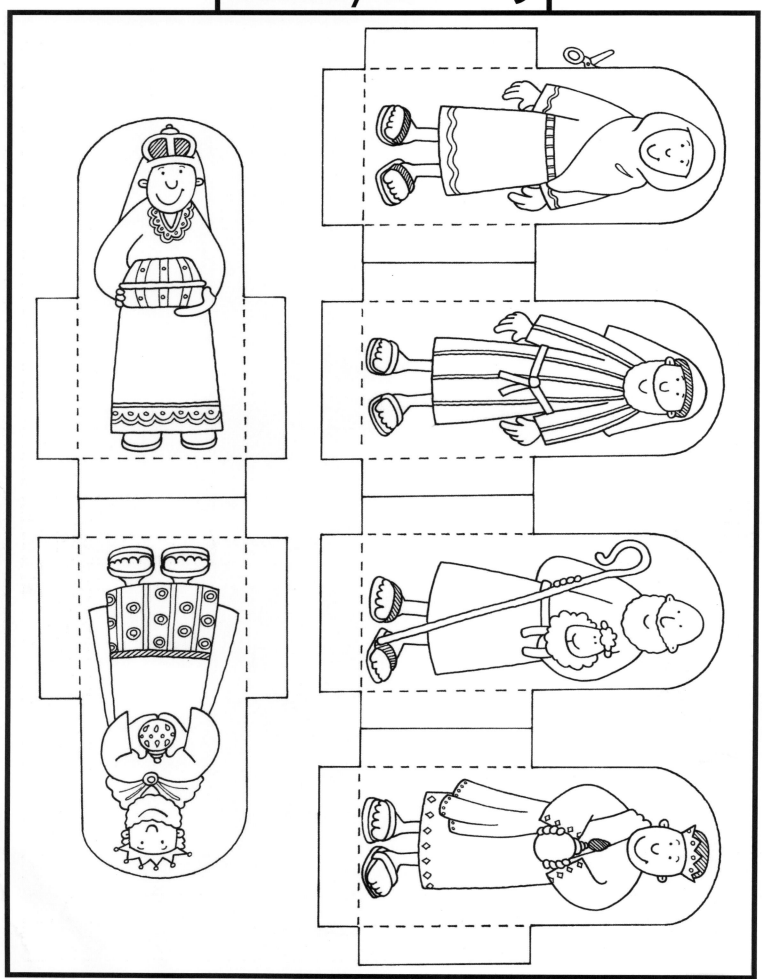

Index

Resources list

This is a list of all of the materials needed to carry out the activities in this pack.

Writing/drawing/painting materials

- Mixing palettes
- Playground chalks
- Coloured crayons
- Coloured pencils
- Ready-mixed paints in a range of colours
- Powder paint red, yellow, white, blue
- Washable felt pens
- Paint brushes
- Water pots

Papers (in a range of colours)

- Sugar paper
- Tissue paper
- Cartridge paper
- Newsprint paper
- Crepe paper
- Shiny/glossy paper
- Card

Craft/modelling/construction materials

- Split pins
- Stapler
- Thin elastic
- Sequins
- Potatoes (for prints)
- Coloured wool scraps
- Blue Tack
- Paper clips
- Tarpaulin
- Rugs
- Benches
- A-frame
- Dowelling
- Large paper plates
- Art straws
- Hole punch
- Safety scissors
- Sticky tape
- Clay/Clay tools
- Large wooden/plastic bricks/crates
- Cotton sheet/calico
- Glue and glue brushes and PVA glue
- Coloured modelling dough
- Coloured threads/ribbons
- Fabric scraps in a variety of colours and patterns

Instruments

- Beaters
- Drums
- Triangles
- Sleigh Bells
- Castanets
- Tambourines

Role play

- Baby doll
- Sponge
- Towel
- Blankets
- Soft toys
- Play people
- Toy vehicles
- Farm animals
- Play food
- Plastic cups, plates, cutlery
- Cash till and coins
- Bags and purses
- Clothes
- Post box/sacks

Investigative

- Magnifying hand lens
- Local greenery
- Fruit and vegetables
- Wrapping paper (with repeated patterns)
- Plastic 2D shapes
- Coloured cellophane
- Torch
- Bubble bath

Other Resources

- Bread
- Margarine
- Honey
- Apples
- Egg
- Flour
- Milk
- Mixing bowl
- Whisk
- Jug
- Plates
- Safety knives and forks
- Small chocolate eggs
- Children's own photos
- Fiction and non-fiction books about new babies
- Art books/posters
- Night light candles
- Dice and counters
- Maps
- Digital camera
- Number line 0-5